GATESHEAD

Architecture in a Changing English Urban Landscape

Published by English Heritage, 23 Savile Row, London W1S 2ET
www.english-heritage.org.uk
English Heritage is the Government's statutory adviser on all aspects of the historic environment.

© English Heritage 2004

Images (except as otherwise shown) © English Heritage or © Crown copyright. NMR.

First published 2004

ISBN 1 873592 76 0
Product code 52000

British Library Cataloguing in Publication Data
A CIP catalogue record for this book is available from the British Library.

Application for the reproduction of images should be made to the National Monuments Record.
Every effort has been made to trace the copyright holders and we apologise in advance for any
unintentional omissions, which we would be pleased to correct in any subsequent edition of this book.

The National Monuments Record is the public archive of English Heritage. For more information
contact NMR Enquiry and Research Services, National Monuments Record Centre, Kemble Drive,
Swindon SN2 2GZ; telephone 01793 414600.

Brought to publication by René Rodgers and Andrew McLaren, Publishing, English Heritage,
Kemble Drive, Swindon SN2 2GZ.

Edited by Delia Gaze
Page layout by George Hammond
Printed in the United Kingdom by Hawthornes

Gateshead Council made a financial contribution towards the publication of this book.

GATESHEAD

Architecture in a Changing English Urban Landscape

Simon Taylor and David B Lovie

Memorial stained-glass window to Joseph Willis and William Swinburne, town clerks of Gateshead from 1856 to 1929, at Gateshead Town Hall, West Street. [AA038868]

Contents

Acknowledgements

The production of this booklet was greatly assisted by the staff of Gateshead Council, especially John Bone, Hugh Martin, Stuart Norman and Geoff Underwood; Anthea Lang and her colleagues at Gateshead Library; and the Chief Archivist and staff of Tyne & Wear Archives Service. Thanks are also due to Bill Fawcett and Frank Manders for invaluable help and information, and to Professor Norman McCord, who commented on the text.

We are also grateful for the assistance and support provided by our colleagues at English Heritage.

The photographs were taken by Bob Skingle and Tony Perry, and Bob Skingle was responsible for the photographic printing. The aerial photographs were taken by Pete Horne and Dave MacLeod. Tony Berry produced the drawings and map. The survey and research for this project were undertaken by Paul Barnwell, Tony Berry, Garry Corbett, Colum Giles, Ian Goodall, Gillian Green, Tony Perry, Bob Skingle, Joanna Smith, Simon Taylor, Andrew Williams and Nicola Wray.

Foreword

The historic environment of England's towns and cities shows the effects of constant change, sometimes slow and almost imperceptible, sometimes radical and plain to see. Whatever the mix, each place shows a distinctive character which reflects its particular development. Some aspects of the historic environment have national or even international significance, others a regional importance; others still are valued as the setting for everyday, local life. The legacy represented by the historic environment is fragile and irreplaceable, and the challenge – for national and local agencies and for people at large – is to identify what is special and to integrate this into sustainable plans for development. The Government's policy of creating urban environments in which people want to live and work will place great pressure on our towns, but it also offers the opportunity of confirming the importance of the historic environment in their future.

The pace of change in Gateshead has been very rapid since the 1990s, particularly on the riverside. Further radical change is imminent as the town adjusts to 21st-century pressures. Renewal will be important, and some of what we see around us today will be replaced by new buildings, designed for a new age. Conspicuous among the challenges facing the town is the Housing Market Renewal Pathfinder initiative, which will produce sustainable communities through a widespread programme of market revival and redevelopment.

Such ambitious plans for change, however, depend for long-term success on more than just economic factors. There is no incompatibility between economic health and a well-presented historic environment, on the contrary. And planning must be informed by a good understanding of the legacy of the past and of the values that local people place upon their surroundings. Both English Heritage and Gateshead Council wish to ensure that the contribution that the historic environment can make to the future of the town – in the quality of life it offers, and in the sense of distinctiveness that is such a powerful source of local pride – is fully considered. Both bodies, therefore, are committed to informed management of change. This publication is offered as a contribution to that process, and it sets out to illustrate the sometimes overlooked aspects of the town's historic fabric, showing how these combine to give Gateshead a strong sense of identity.

Sir Neil Cossons
Chairman, English Heritage

Councillor Mick Henry
Leader, Gateshead Council

CHAPTER 1

Topography, industry and economy

Situated on the south bank of the River Tyne and perennially overshadowed by its mighty neighbour Newcastle, Gateshead, often paralleled with Southwark in terms of its relationship with London, has, for most of its history, been overlooked, undervalued and often misunderstood. It was dismissed in the 1930s by J B Priestley in his *English Journey* as a huge dingy dormitory, inferior even to the constructions of insects, and the modern traveller from the south is safely channelled past most of Gateshead, either by the busy and often re-routed bypass roads or by a rail route that does not provide a station until Newcastle itself is reached. Yet between the twin jewels of the *Angel of the North* and BALTIC The Centre for Contemporary Art lie a town and borough with a history that offers a fascinating insight into urban development and planning in England over the last two centuries. The buildings of Gateshead are at once a microcosm of most urban English building trends and an interesting example of regional diversification, as the local and sometimes national authorities struggled to overcome successive social, economic and industrial challenges. The result is a highly distinctive historic built environment.

Until the onset of the Industrial Revolution, Gateshead had existed for centuries as a small and obscure river and roadside town (Fig 1), its prosperity based primarily on the all-important coal trade. Coal mining in the area began in the 14th century, promoted by the Bishop of Durham, who was quick to realise the importance of the mineral wealth beneath the town. It reached its peak during the 17th century and then slowly declined, although the last pit, Redheugh, did not finally close until 1927. The landscape was extensively scarred by the detritus of mining and was criss-crossed by mineral railways taking coal from the pits to the river, but there is little obvious trace to be seen above ground today. The true legacy of so many years of mining activity is a vast subterranean network of shafts and galleries that have helped to shape much of Gateshead's modern urban landscape.

Like many towns, Gateshead was transformed by the Industrial Revolution. Fuelled by the local coal, a variety of new industries developed, in particular chemicals, iron founding and locomotive manufacture, that radically changed the face of the town. The arrival of

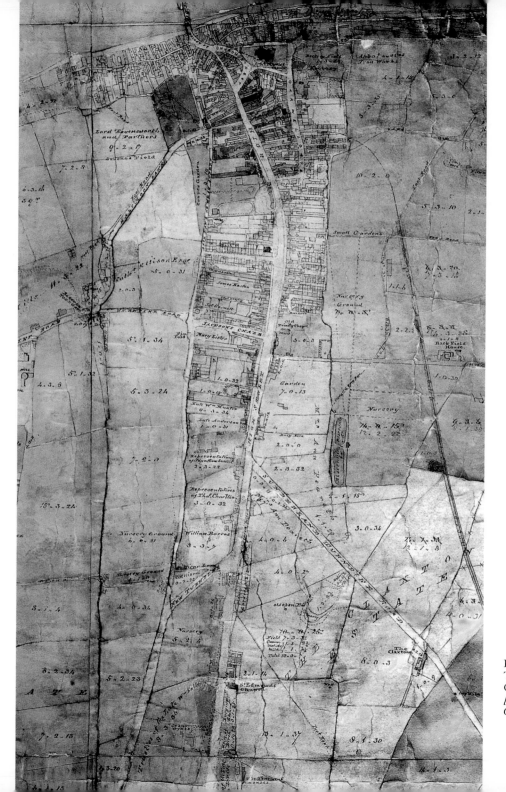

Fig 1 *John Bell's plan of*
The Borough of Gateshead in the
County of Durham, *1835.*
*[Reproduced courtesy of Gateshead
Council; DP000121]*

a host of new workers caused rapid population increase, from 8,597 in 1801 to 85,692 in 1891. That tenfold increase caused a severe housing shortage still felt in the later 20th century. Gateshead was a 19th-century boom town; it gained its own MP in 1832, became a municipal borough in 1835 and a county borough in 1889. (It remained a county borough until merger with Blaydon, Felling, Ryton, Whickham, Birtley and Lamesley formed Gateshead Metropolitan Borough in 1973/4.) The industries that sustained the town throughout the 19th century and into the 20th, however, were already in decline by the 1880s and finally failed with the recession of the inter-war period. The iron-founders Hawks Crawshay & Sons, the makers of High Level Bridge, for example, had provided the economic backbone of the town during the first half of the 19th century but had closed by 1889, and John Abbot & Co at Park Works, neighbours and rivals of Hawks', followed in 1909. Both manufacturers suffered because they had failed to specialise in a particular product and became uncompetitive. Fortunately, by then the locomotive works of the North Eastern Railway at Greenesfield, the only substantial relic of the industrial era in Gateshead, was able to provide mass employment for the town, at least for a while. Interestingly, the Greenesfield site did not start as a manufacturing facility, and indeed the location of the works is largely the outcome of accident rather than of careful planning, a factor that was to contribute to its downfall nearly seventy years later.

Greene's Field was first developed for railway use in the early 1840s when it effectively became the Newcastle station of the Newcastle and Darlington Junction Railway. Because the Tyne gorge was too steep to cross viably at that time, a short-lived passenger station was built on the site in 1844 to designs by the York architect George Townsend Andrews. Part of this structure survived until it was dismantled in 2003 (Fig 2). The opening of Robert Stephenson's High Level Bridge in 1849, which at a stroke overcame the obstacle represented by the gorge, and the construction of Newcastle Central Station, opened in 1850, rendered Greenesfield station redundant. The site was developed instead as a locomotive repair works, and in 1854 it became the main locomotive works of the newly formed North Eastern Railway (NER). The works expanded fairly steadily, reaching its fullest practical extent about 1900 (Fig 3). By 1909 it was the largest single employer in Gateshead, with more than 3,300 workers. Ironically, it was at this point that the lack of space at the limited site, originally chosen for convenience, proved critical. The 20th century brought with it the need for a new and larger type of more powerful locomotive. Locomotive manufacture was moved to Darlington in 1910, and Greenesfield was maintained as a repair facility until it was closed by the London and North Eastern Railway in 1932. This did not mean the demolition of the works, but subsequent activity on the site was limited; the works reopened during the Second World War for repair work and remained in general use until 1959, the engine shed being rebuilt by British Railways in 1956. It was last used by the English Welsh & Scottish Railway (EWS) as a maintenance facility, before falling into disuse towards the end of the 20th century.

The failure of traditional industry in Gateshead was part of the much bigger story of industrial decline and economic recession that gripped the country in the 1920s. The north-east of England, dependent on coal mining, shipbuilding and a few other intensive heavy industries, was one of the hardest-hit areas. The social problems that followed were expressed in the 'Jarrow Crusade' of 1936. The situation became so critical that the government intervened to encourage new industries in the region. This was quite new in Britain: never before had central government considered putting so much public resource – nearly £2,000,000, awarded under the Special Areas (Development and Improvement) Act of 1934 – into economic regeneration, although in reality the scale of the problem rather dwarfed its significance. The emphasis was on light industry, diversification and, for once, a clean, pleasant and well-planned industrial environment. The result was the Team Valley Trading Estate (TVTE), a massive undertaking, intended to provide employment for 15,000 workers within fifteen years. It was masterminded by William G Holford under Colonel Kenelm C Appleyard, formerly of the Birtley Iron and Engineering Works, who headed a new company, North Eastern Trading Estates Ltd (NETE). Construction work began in 1936, and the estate was formally opened by King George VI three years later.

Fig 2 *Former station hotel, 1844, at Greenesfield by G T Andrews of York; it was dismantled in 2003. The later engineering workshops can be seen on the right of this view. [AA028727]*

NORTH-EASTERN RAILWAY WORKS, GATESHEAD—GENERAL PLAN

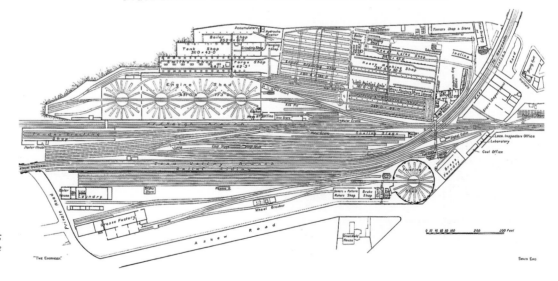

Fig 3 *North Eastern Railway Works at Greenesfield. Andrews' former station hotel is shown as the pay office. [From* The Engineer, *18 December 1896, 608; Science Museum/Science & Society Picture Library]*

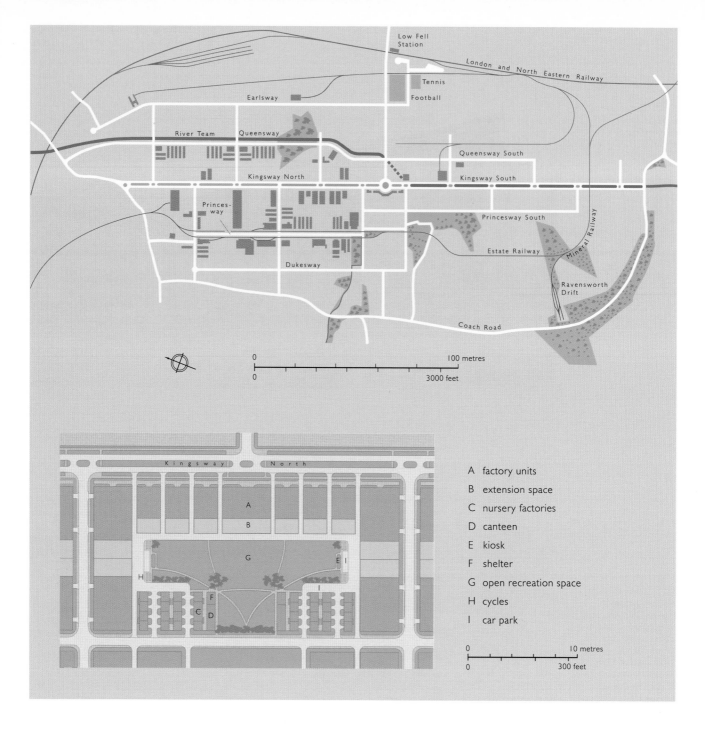

Low Fell
Station

London and North Eastern Railway

Tennis

Football

Earlsway

River Team   Queensway

Queensway South

Kingsway North

Kingsway South

Princes-
way

Princesway South

Estate Railway

Dukesway

Mineral Railway

Ravensworth
Drift

Coach Road

0   100 metres

0   3000 feet

Kingsway   North

A

B

G

E I

H

F

C D

I

A factory units

B extension space

C nursery factories

D canteen

E kiosk

F shelter

G open recreation space

H cycles

I car park

0   10 metres

0   300 feet

Fig 4 *The Team Valley Trading Estate in 1939. Inset: how it was expected that factory communities would develop.*

Fig 5 *An artist's impression of the headquarters building of North Eastern Trading Estates Ltd, presented in 1937 when the foundation stone was laid. [AA0028894]*

It is easy to forget the significance of the TVTE. Its architecture is modest, its layout more suburban than heroic, but the contrast with what had gone before and the boldness of the experiment – it was intended to bring social stability and a new economic base to the area – should not be overlooked. Nearly two miles (3.2km) long, it was the size of a small town, with what was then one of the widest roads in the country, Kingsway (which included the canalised River Team running in the middle of the southern half), as its spine. The estate was attractively landscaped; football pitches were laid out on vacant parts; and it was hoped that its park-like appearance would engender leisure use (Fig 4). At the centre NETE built for itself an extensive, crescent-shaped headquarters with detached blocks containing a bank and a post office (Fig 5). Factories were provided in three standard sizes (Figs 6, 7 and 8), the largest of 14,085 sq ft (1,308.5 sq m), and some bespoke factories were also built for individual companies. Of particular significance was the provision of so-called 'nursery' factories of 1,500 sq ft (139.5 sq m) each, built in blocks of four. Available for a weekly

inclusive rent of only £1, they were intended to nurture small industrial ventures without much capital, which, if successful, could move on into larger units. Many of the first factories built at TVTE were tenanted, with the encouragement of the government, by central and east European refugees escaping from oppression on the Continent.

The Second World War of 1939–45 largely halted expansion, and most of the factories were turned to war production. When the war was over, commercial building started again and a number of good-quality bespoke factories were erected. Among the best of them were a specially designed plant for Sigmund Pumps (founded in 1937 by a Czechoslovakian refugee, Miroslav Sigmund) on Queensway, by Yorke, Rosenberg and Mardall, in 1948, and a factory on Kingsway for Armstrong Cork, by D McIntyre, also of 1948. Notable later developments included the two-phase processed cheese plant built by Kavli of Norway (1957 and 1961) on Kingsway and the British Road Services depot on Earlsway.

The initial success of the TVTE is difficult to judge. Factory take-up was swift and plentiful (110 tenant firms had registered by the end of 1939, employing nearly 5,000 people), but much of the huge area remained unused for a long time and the almost immediate outbreak of the Second World War brought with it a new set of economic conditions and priorities. The target of 15,000 workers was not achieved in peacetime until the 1960s. Today, most of the vacant plots on the estate have been built upon and the activities are as diverse as Appleyard could have wished. A handful of first-generation factories survive, as does NETE's original headquarters, and a few, such as Loblite Ltd on Third Avenue (founded in 1939 by the Loebl Brothers), still have their original occupiers. The emphasis, however, has changed, and the TVTE is now home to many modern high-tech industries in new buildings and has by far the largest concentration of employers in Gateshead. With the turn of the millennium, Gateshead, the old 'workman's town', has once again re-invented itself from within and raised its profile, developing as a centre of sporting excellence and earning an enviable reputation as an internationally important cultural centre.

Fig 6 (above, top) A standard factory of 8,000 sq ft (743.2 sq m) on First Avenue. The two-storeyed office block provided a frontage to the factory proper, which was lit from the side walls and by clerestory windows. [DP00043]

Fig 7 (above, bottom) Block I.60.a–d, a standard block of four 'nursery' factories on Third Avenue occupied by Loblite, an electrical accessories company established at the Team Valley Trading Estate in 1939 by the German-Jewish refugee brothers Fritz S and Robert Loebl. [DP00042]

Fig 8 (right) Plans and elevation of a standard 8,000-square-foot (743.2-square-metre) factory (above) and of a standard block of four or two nursery factories (below).

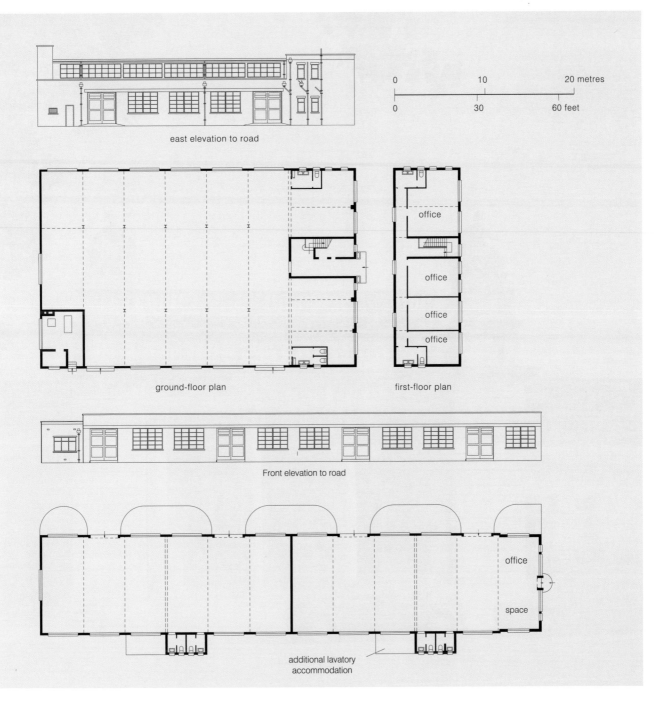

east elevation to road

0   10   20 metres

0   30   60 feet

ground-floor plan

first-floor plan

office

office

office

office

Front elevation to road

office

space

additional lavatory
accommodation

CHAPTER 2

Public Buildings

The tremendous development of Gateshead during the 19th and 20th centuries raised important questions about how the town should be governed. A municipal borough was created in 1835, but initially its functions were limited to raising rates and such things as the upkeep of the roads and the Night Watch. Further roles were later added, including responsibility for health (1848), sanitary conditions (1872) and education (1902). The authorities were perpetually hampered by the limited income that could be raised from the low rateable value of the property in the town and by the fickle nature of central government support. Nevertheless, they strove to house themselves in buildings that were not merely functional, but made a positive statement about the collective image, aspirations and culture of the borough's inhabitants.

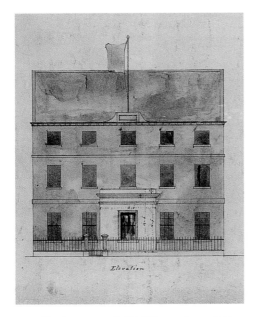

Fig 9 *The former town hall building at Greenesfield, demolished in 1867. [TWAS/T429, reproduced by permission of the Chief Archivist, Tyne & Wear Archives Service; AA040376]*

Housing the council

Local government in Gateshead occupied a succession of buildings. When the newly elected Borough Council of Gateshead first met, at the end of 1835, it did so in a solicitor's office and continued in temporary accommodation until a house on the west side of Oakwellgate was rented to serve as town hall and police house. Then, in 1844, an attractive three-storeyed house at Greenesfield, close to the new railway station, was acquired and converted for use as a town hall (Fig 9), and a new police station appears to have been built alongside. It was probably expected that the locality was destined to become the new town centre, a honeypot for trade and administration, and the focus for travellers to and from the south. In the event the extension of the railway line to Newcastle, the closure of the station at Greenesfield and the subsequent building of the railway works left the town hall marooned in unsuitable surroundings. Nevertheless, the council remained there until early 1867, when it was forced to yield the land to the NER. By then, however, plans for an entirely new town hall, on land near Swinburne Place between High Street and West Street, were already well underway.

In 1863 a competition for a design for a new town hall had been won by John Johnstone, the architect of Newcastle Town Hall, with the second prize going to Edward Watson. The Town Surveyor was duly instructed to produce a design embodying the best elements of each. The project was immediately beset by problems. There were arguments as to whether the building should face High or West Street, and it was not until 1865 that plans for a High Street town hall, estimated at a colossal £22,300, were agreed. The scheme ran into trouble when excavations for the foundations penetrated the partially worked High Main Coal Seam, incidentally causing the partial collapse of some properties in Nelson Street. Work appears to have ceased, and the displaced town council took up temporary residence, along with the County Court Judge, at the Queen's Head Inn. Designs for a West Street town hall were then invited and Johnstone was appointed as architect; this time the building was to cost no more than £12,000. Work began in 1867 and was completed to budget in January 1870 (Figs 10 and 11). The building not only accommodated the town

Fig 11 *The opulent entrance hall of the Town Hall on West Street. [AA038608]*

Fig 12 *A plan of the ground floor of the Town Hall on West Street, dated 1868, showing the many different activities that the building was to house. The roofed area to the left of the police cells was the fire-engine house. [TWAS/T429, reproduced by permission of the Chief Archivist, Tyne & Wear Archives Service; AA040370]*

Fig 13 *The lower cell corridor at the former police station, Gateshead Town Hall. There was a similar corridor on the floor above. [AA038570]*

council but was an extensive complex housing a variety of municipal services (Fig 12). This saved much time in the days before telephones. The 'town hall' also contained a police station (which included cells, Fig 13, with drill yard and a fire-engine house, because at that time policemen were also firemen), the magistrates' and county courts, and a large public hall with first- and second-class refreshment rooms. The building was Italianate in style and two storeys high over a basement. The front elevation displayed symbols of the town including goat's-head reliefs and, originally, the figures of *Commerce*, *Industry* and *Justice*, surmounted by a statue of *Queen Victoria*. Gateshead Town Hall was a fairly typical example of a mid-19th-century small town hall. It lacks the grandeur and scale of big-city contemporaries, such as Leeds and Manchester, but as the first purpose-built structure of its kind in the borough it must have seemed a magnificent achievement for such a comparatively impoverished town.

The West Street town hall was built at the height of the town council's authority and provided a strong symbol of civic pride and ambition. (At the laying of the foundation stone the crowds had been so great that a stand collapsed, causing a fatality.) It continued to serve the council into the 1980s, the public hall being converted into the council chamber (probably in 1973/4, when the metropolitan borough was created), but by then council business had outgrown the accommodation provided in Johnstone's building. An entirely new civic centre for Gateshead was first proposed immediately after the Second World War, and a handsome new Borough Treasurer's Department at Shipcote opened in 1954, described as 'Civic Centre First Stage' (Fig 14). It had a circular single-storeyed ratings hall at the south end (Fig 15) and an adjacent two-storeyed office block, which was heightened to three storeys in the early 1970s. Despite this fine start, Shipcote was not destined to become the new administrative focal point of the borough. Instead, a new civic centre finally opened in 1987, on Regent Street, in an area with civic character already expressed in the police headquarters of 1972 and magistrates' court of 1976 (Fig 16). The large and sprawling Civic Centre is perhaps out of proportion with its surroundings; the three-storeyed central square block (containing a

Fig 14 *(left) The Borough Treasurer's Department (Civic Centre First Stage), Prince Consort Road, was opened in 1954. The third storey was added between 1972 and 1974 by A Leslie Berry, the Borough Architect. [AA038565]*

Fig 15 *(below) The interior of the ratings hall, Gateshead Borough Treasurer's Department. [AA038589]*

Fig 16 *(below) Gateshead Civic Centre, Regent Street, opened in 1987. [DP000118]*

Fig 17 *(right) The council chamber, Gateshead Civic Centre. Two of the four stained-glass panels of 1986 that make up* The Gateshead Story *can be seen on the right. [AA038665]*

full-height galleried public circulation area) is supplemented by council departments housed in quadrangular blocks, one projecting from each corner. The council chamber (Fig 17) is notable for its four stained-glass panels, *The Gateshead Story*, by the architect D W Robson and inspired by the glass in the old town hall. It was hoped that every citizen of the borough would find his or her life represented somewhere in the panels, which depict the past and present character of the borough, with the River Tyne, represented at the bottom of each, as the connecting theme.

Hospitals and schools

The hospitals and schools built by the Gateshead authorities tell a story that is common to many towns and cities in England. Little survives from the early period of ad hoc local provision, and later structures, which were highly functional, have been subject to development and improvement where they have not been demolished.

Fig 18 *The house on Nelson Street that served as Gateshead Dispensary from 1855 to 1946. [AA038585]*

Fig 19 *The former Gateshead Borough Lunatic Asylum (Later St Mary's Hospital), designed by G T Hine in 1910, from the south. [AA041013]*

Fig 20 *Bensham Hospital was originally built between 1886 and 1890 as the infirmary of Gateshead Union Workhouse. This view shows the central administration block and one of the ward pavilions. [AA040273]*

Most of Gateshead's historic hospital buildings have been demolished, their functions now being absorbed within a single general hospital. Still standing are the 1830s mansion on Nelson Street that housed the town's dispensary (founded in 1832 following a cholera outbreak in 1831) from 1855 to 1946 (Fig 18), and Gateshead's first purpose-built hospital, Sheriff Hill Isolation Hospital, built in 1880. Similarly intact is the large, sprawling Gateshead Borough Lunatic Asylum, for pauper lunatics, built well outside Gateshead in an isolated spot near Stannington in Northumberland. Latterly known as Gateshead Mental Hospital, then St Mary's Hospital and now closed, it was designed by G T Hine in 1910 for 400–500 inmates and is a splendid example of an early 20th-century municipal lunatic asylum (Fig 19). The first general hospital was Bensham Hospital (Fig 20). Originally built between 1886 and 1890 as the infirmary of Gateshead Union Workhouse, it was converted into a general hospital in 1941, following a review of health services in the borough and an influx of war wounded. At the same time work was underway on the Queen Elizabeth

Fig 21 *The isolation block at the Queen Elizabeth Hospital, built in the years 1938–40. [AA040361]*

Hospital, a new general hospital. Designed by F H Patterson with the guidance of the chief architect H J Cook, construction began in June 1939 and the hospital was finally opened in March 1948. The original brick buildings are architecturally modest. A three-storeyed multi-purpose main block housed the outpatients' department, general wards, operating suite and X-ray department, plus offices, kitchen and stores. There was also a single-storeyed maternity unit and a new isolation hospital (Fig 21), the latter in a detached position close to the main gate with its pair of lodges. Services (laundry, etc) were housed in a complex of buildings between the main block and the new isolation hospital. The role of the hospital has increased in importance since its completion and it has been enlarged and remodelled several times.

Of the many neighbourhood board schools built under the authority of the Elementary Education Act of 1870, only a few, such as the Day Industrial Schools at Windmill Hills (1878–80, by Thomas Oliver) and Wrekenton School (1899–1900) at the southern end of the borough, survive in substantial form (Figs 22 and 23). A second great period of school building began with the growth of council-housing estates in the 1920s and 1930s, and saw the construction of schools such as Carr Hill (1927–30) and St Wilfrid's Roman Catholic School at Old Fold.

Fig 22 *(right, top) The former Day Industrial School for Girls and Boys, Windmill Hills, designed by Thomas Oliver in 1878 and opened in 1880. The lower part to the left was the infant school. [AA040354]*

Fig 23 *(right, bottom) Wrekenton School was built in 1899. It is much smaller and less imposing than the school at Windmill Hills. [AA040352]*

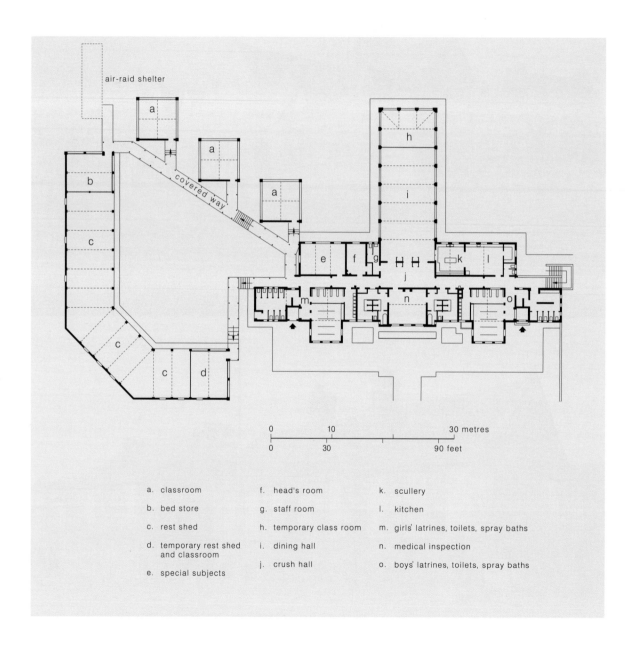

air-raid shelter

a

b

c

c

c d

covered way

a

a

h

i

e f g

j

k l

m

n

o

0	10		30 metres
0	30		90 feet

a. classroom

b. bed store

c. rest shed

d. temporary rest shed
   and classroom

e. special subjects

f. head's room

g. staff room

h. temporary class room

i. dining hall

j. crush hall

k. scullery

l. kitchen

m. girls' latrines, toilets, spray baths

n. medical inspection

o. boys' latrines, toilets, spray baths

Fig 24 *(left) Joicey Road Open-Air School as it was designed in 1936. Although it was first suggested in 1924, the school did not open until 1937; the air-raid shelter was added during the war years.*

Fig 25 *(above) Most of the teaching at Joicey Road Open-Air School would have been conducted in the open, except in poor weather when these classroom pavilions would have been used. All the windows are designed to open fully, as is shown in this view of 1937. [Reproduced courtesy of Gateshead Council; AA040449]*

This period also saw the building of one of Gateshead's hidden gems, the Joicey Road Open-Air School for 'sickly' children, proposed in 1924 but not opened until 1937 (Fig 24). This is a rare and well-preserved, if late, example of an open-air school in England, one of a number built in the 1920s and 1930s. They were based on a school of 1904 at Charlottenburg near Berlin, which was copied in London by 1907, and mostly admitted children with tuberculosis. Fresh air was considered to be all-important, and teaching and afternoon naps were conducted outdoors, the buildings being for use only in poor weather, for meals and medical inspections (Fig 25).

Fig 26 *Gateshead Technical College on Durham Road was built between 1949 and 1955. [DP00045]*

The open-air school was followed in 1946 by the opening of a school for 'educationally sub-normal children' outside the borough at Hindley Hall, an earlier building specially extended for the purpose by Gateshead's Borough Surveyor. Facilities for adult education were also improved with the building of Gateshead Technical College (1949–55, Fig 26), which replaced a pair of 19th-century villas on the same site that had been converted for the purpose in the 1930s. The end of the war also saw an ambitious new programme of general school building, executed over the next few decades. A good example is Dryden Road Girls' Grammar School, opened in 1956 (Fig 27). The following year, Gateshead joined with other local authorities to form the Consortium of Local Authorities Special Programme (CLASP) and adopted a system of pre-fabricated school building, originally designed for use in Nottinghamshire. This was quick, cheap, simple and, equally importantly, suitable for use in areas prone to mining subsidence, because its pin-jointed method of construction meant that the buildings could flex with ground movements. The CLASP system has been used

Fig 27 *The former Girls' Grammar School, Dryden Road. It opened in 1956. [AA041011]*

for most Gateshead schools built since the 1950s. One of the early examples was Breckenbeds Middle School, Saltwell Road South, built in 1963/4 in CLASP mark 3B. It has recently been extended in CLASP mark 6B and converted into the Joseph Swan secondary school. The new building deliberately echoes the adult workplace, resembling a corporate headquarters and reflecting those at the nearby Team Valley Trading Estate. It is now run as a specialist technology college, by the Technology Colleges Trust, demonstrating the borough's (and the government's) continuing emphasis on vocational education and the influence of the town's industrial past.

Arts and libraries

The story of permanent public arts and libraries in Gateshead begins with the public library built on Swinburne Street that opened in 1885

(Figs 28 and 29). The passing of the Public Libraries Act thirty years earlier in 1855 had permitted local authorities to raise a penny rate for the provision of buildings and books, but it was not until 1880 that a meeting of the burgesses of Gateshead was called to determine whether to adopt it. The delay was mainly due to the council's reluctance to agree to the rate, but also partly because of opposition from the Mechanics' Institute, which opposed the free library movement. The burgesses voted narrowly in favour, and John Johnstone was appointed to design and build a new library behind the town hall. Work began in 1882 and was completed in 1885, after Johnstone's death. Built on a shoestring, Johnstone's small baroque library combined a first-floor art school and gallery (*see* Fig 33a) with ground-floor public reading rooms and book department. It was built before the general introduction of today's open-access system, and readers had to consult a catalogue and ask for individual volumes at a counter. Availability was logged by means of a 12,000-book Cotgreave indicator, a large frame containing a mini ledger for each book, recording its loan status. The library proved immensely popular, soon reaching capacity in terms of users, and within twenty years was already considered too small, forcing the council to start thinking about an alternative.

In 1909, before ideas for a new library had been formulated, Joseph Aynsley Davidson Shipley, a wealthy Newcastle solicitor and an enthusiastic, if ill-informed, art collector, died, leaving his vast and varied art collection to the City of Newcastle along with £30,000 to build a new gallery for it. Newcastle refused the offer, because many of the paintings were copies, and under the terms of the will the collection was offered to Gateshead. Even in an impoverished town like Gateshead, however, official opinion was split as to whether the bequest should be accepted, Lord Northbourne (a major local landowner) describing the collection as 'quasi cast-off clothes'. Eventually, however, the offer of £30,000 and the prospect of a brand new art gallery proved irresistible, and the Shipley Art Gallery was built between 1914 and 1917 at Shipcote (Figs 30 and 31; *see also* 33b). Designed by the Newcastle architect Arthur Stockwell, it is an elegant building in an Edwardian baroque style. Unlike the gallery and studios above the

Fig 28 *(left) The former Public Library on Swinburne Street. It was designed by John Johnstone and built between 1882 and 1885. [AA041012]*

Fig 29 *Former Public Library, Swinburne Street. The library itself occupied only the ground floor and basement; the first floor contained an art school and gallery. [TWAS/T429, reproduced by permission of the Chief Archivist, Tyne & Wear Archives Service; AA040365]*

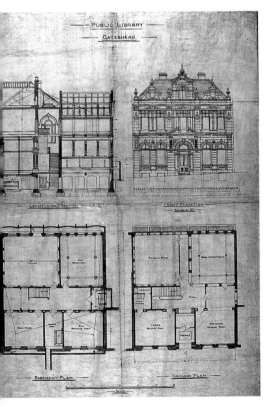

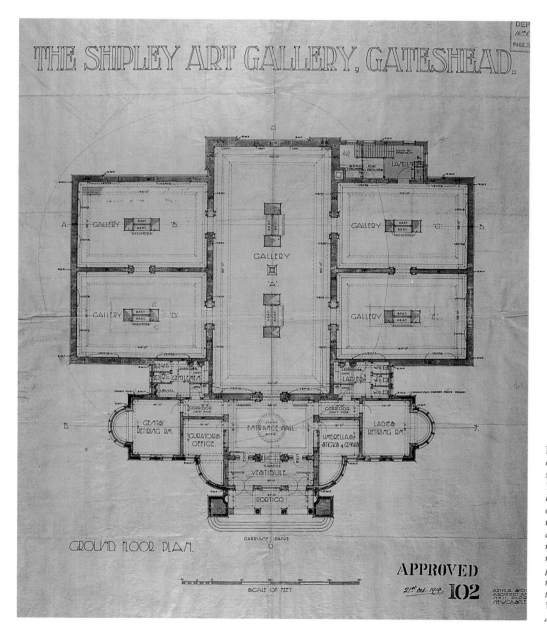

Fig 30 *Ground-floor plan
of the Shipley Art Gallery,
submitted in October 1914.
The layout of the gallery
has changed little but many
of the fittings have been
removed; only galleries 'B'
and 'D' (on this plan)
retain their seats and
radiators.
[TWAS/T311/102/1914,
reproduced by permission of
the Chief Archivist, Tyne &
Wear Archives Service;
AA040378]*

Fig 31 *The Shipley Art Gallery, Prince Consort Road, was designed by Arthur Stockwell of Newcastle and built in the years 1914–17. [AA038558]*

Fig 32 *The Public Library, Prince Consort Road, was designed by Arthur Stockwell and (after Stockwell's death) David Ditchburn. It was built in 1925/6 with the aid of a grant of £16,500 from the Carnegie Trust. [AA038543]*

library in Swinburne Street, there were no windows in the side walls, since the display spaces were originally top-lit by corrugated roof lights designed for an even diffusion of light. Its controversial beginnings aside, the gallery remains an elegant and attractive building that graces its location and has proved itself, in many ways, to be an asset to the town.

The problem of the library appeared to have been solved at much the same time as the building of the gallery, when in 1916 the Carnegie Trust of Dunfermline offered Gateshead a grant of £15,000 for a new public library. No action was taken by the council, however, until the end of the First World War in 1918, when Arthur Stockwell was again appointed as architect. Initial designs were costed at far more than the proffered grant, even though it was raised to £16,500, and a period of inactivity followed, during which Stockwell died. Activity was again stimulated when the Carnegie Trust threatened to withdraw its offer, and, in 1925/6, a reduced design was executed by David Ditchburn with a top-up loan of £6,500 from the government (Fig 32). The Public Library was also built at Shipcote, away from the town centre and so helping to refocus the town's civic heart, and its design clearly echoes that of its neighbour, the Shipley Art Gallery. Unlike its predecessor of 1885, it was operated on the open-access system. It has served Gateshead well, being extended in 1975/6 by Leslie Berry, the Borough Architect, and remains the town's main library.

In the early 1980s the lack of a contemporary art gallery prompted Gateshead Council to commission a number of pieces of public art. This initiative gained momentum, and an enviable national reputation, over the next fifteen years. It reached a high-water mark with Antony Gormley's *Angel of the North* in 1998 (Fig 33c). Equally innovative, and doing even more to consolidate Gateshead's association with the arts, was the opening of BALTIC The Centre for Contemporary Art in July 2002. The Centre is contained within a former grain warehouse, originally part of Joseph Rank Ltd Baltic Flour Mills, beside the River Tyne. Built in 1950, the mills were designed by Mouchel and Partners and processed imported wheat both for baking and for animal feed; when opened they had a silo capacity of 20,000 tonnes. Most of the

a

b

c

d

Fig 33 *The changing face of art in Gateshead:*
(a) the light and airy 'museum painting room' (1885) above the public library
in Swinburne Street [AA038641];
(b) Edwardian restraint at the Shipley Art Gallery (1917) [AA038621];
(c) the gritty and monumental Angel of the North *(1998) [AA09246]; and*
(d) the conceptual BALTIC (2002) [AA040383].

Fig 34 *The former grain warehouse of Joseph Rank Ltd Baltic Flour Mills, by Mouchel and Partners, of 1950, which reopened in July 2002 as BALTIC The Centre for Contemporary Art. Behind it, the towers of Baltic Quay, a mixed residential and leisure development, can be seen under construction.* [AA040390]

complex was demolished after the mills were closed in the early 1980s, leaving only the gauntly functional grain warehouse beside the river. The potential of the site, and the need to regenerate the river frontage, prompted Gateshead Council and the Royal Institute of British Architects (RIBA) to invite designs to convert the surviving building into an arts exhibition facility. The competition was won by Dominic Williams, and in 1998/9 the warehouse was stripped to only its façades and rebuilt as an 'art factory' with six main floors and three mezzanines (Fig 33d). Together with Gateshead's Millennium Bridge, BALTIC has become something of an icon, its unorthodox installations provoking much public debate, and the focus for Gateshead Quays, a new residential and cultural centre at the north end of the town (Fig 34). The riverside development, which includes The Sage Gateshead, a pioneering new music centre by Norman Foster, has helped to win Gateshead and Newcastle collectively international recognition as a centre of cultural vitality.

CHAPTER 3

Housing

The provision of housing in Gateshead developed in different stages during the 19th and 20th centuries and shows how private developers and public authorities grappled with high population growth and grave overcrowding problems. The type and location of housing produced at different periods have been influenced by changing economic circumstances and by evolving trends in housing theory and philosophy. Gateshead's housing stock reflects both the national trends that dominate the period and a strong local character, the result of local housing tradition, local priorities, land availability and local personalities. What is left is a rich housing legacy, part microcosm of the history of mass housing in England, part unmistakably of the region.

Bensham and Shipcote, 1800–1914

In the period from the beginning of the 19th century until the outbreak of the First World War, Gateshead was transformed from a small riverside trading town into a sprawling industrial borough. The poorest of the growing population were at first crammed into the town's historic centre, either side of the High Street and on the slopes of the river banks (Fig 35). The insanitary housing conditions and the increasingly industrial character of the riverside town drove the wealthier classes out to Bensham, the first suburb, but later Bensham and the area around it were developed intensely for the working classes. By 1914 almost all of the area had been built upon and the locality today is characterised by street after street of well-spaced, low- to middle-quality housing. The old working-class housing has been cleared from the town centre, but 19th- and early 20th-century Bensham and Shipcote remain largely intact, and the historical development of the area can still be traced clearly through its architecture.

At the start of the 19th century the Bensham area, called the town fields, was a tract of ancient common, and the land to the immediate south and east was mainly part of the Shipcote Estate. The area came under pressure as population grew, and in 1814 an Act was passed

Fig 35 *Pipewellgate and Rabbit Banks in 1925.*
[Reproduced courtesy of Gateshead Council;
AA040447]

permitting the enclosure and fragmentation of the town fields. In 1818
they were divided among the borough-holders (owners of certain
properties in the original medieval part of the town to which certain
borough rights were attached), many of whom built themselves fine new
houses, or sold their plots to others for building. A select and semi-rural
suburb developed with dispersed dwellings in the form of villas, such as
Woodbine Cottage (Fig 36) and Barrington Villa, some built and
occupied by wealthy merchants from Newcastle. Isolated terraces were
also erected and were occupied by private gentlemen and by Gateshead
tradesmen and merchants, whose businesses remained in the old
town centre. The first of these terraces was probably Claremont Place
(Fig 37), which was built in phases between 1819 and 1824 on land
belonging to William Hymers, a local iron master. Nos 1–10 were
evidently built as one planned development. The houses are of stone
with muted classical detailing, ashlar to the front, random rubble to the
rear. They are two storeys high over service basements and have small

Fig 36 *(above left) Woodbine Cottage, Villa Place, a house with fine architectural detail. When it was built this elevation faced landscaped gardens. [AA041014]*

Fig 37 *(above right) Nos 1–9 Claremont Place were built between 1819 and 1824 and originally faced open farmland. The good ashlar and restrained classical detail of the façades give way to simple rubble stone at the rear. [AA036743]*

rear service yards but long front gardens, an arrangement characteristic of many of Bensham's early semi-rural terraces. Barrington Place, originally a row of five stone houses, had also been built by 1824, and in 1833 its residents included the master of the Anchorage School, Gateshead, a general merchant with business premises at Quayside, Newcastle, and at least two private gentlemen.

By the early 1830s more terraces had been built, including Woodbine Terrace, a phased development of eighteen houses, some of stone and some of brick, with long front gardens and small rear yards. The Honeysuckle Hotel at 1 Woodbine Terrace, extensively rebuilt and enlarged in the early 20th century, was in existence in 1850 and may have been built as an inn, reflecting the increasing needs of the growing community. Sedgewick Place, another development of this period, is a row of eight houses of two storeys over raised basements. These houses have brick fronts, with gardens, and face westwards, overlooking Claremont Place. The rears are of random stone rubble and backed onto Coatsworth Road, then called Union Lane. Latterly, however, with the development of Coatsworth Road as a shopping street, the Sedgewick Place houses have effectively been reversed,

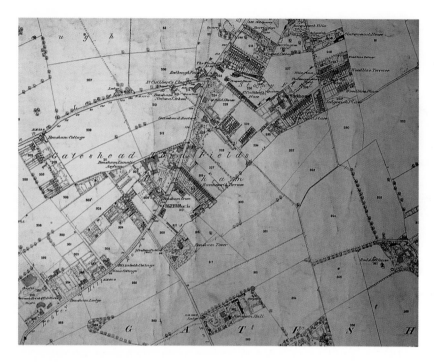

Fig 38 *(left) Ordnance Survey map showing part of Bensham in the mid-1850s. It is still very rural in character. [Reproduced courtesy of Gateshead Council from the Ordnance Survey map of 1855/6; DP000120]*

Fig 39 *(right) Ordnance Survey map showing part of Bensham in 1914, now largely built up. [Reproduced from the 1919 Ordnance Survey map; AA040910]*

and single-storeyed shops, fronting Coatsworth Road, have been built over their former rear yards.

In the mid-19th century the character of Bensham was still that of a dispersed semi-rural suburb of the middle classes (Fig 38). Housing development had been slow and piecemeal, since only relatively small areas of land at a time were released for building and then they were rarely developed in one go or to any large scheme. All this was soon to change, however, because in the second half of the century population pressure, and the potential financial opportunities for landlords, rapidly increased the demand for more housing beyond the old town. By 1900 the area had substantially changed in character; it was almost fully built up and had become predominantly a working-class and lower-middle-class zone (Fig 39).

In general, Bensham was developed from north to south, but the development of individual streets was usually piecemeal. Although land

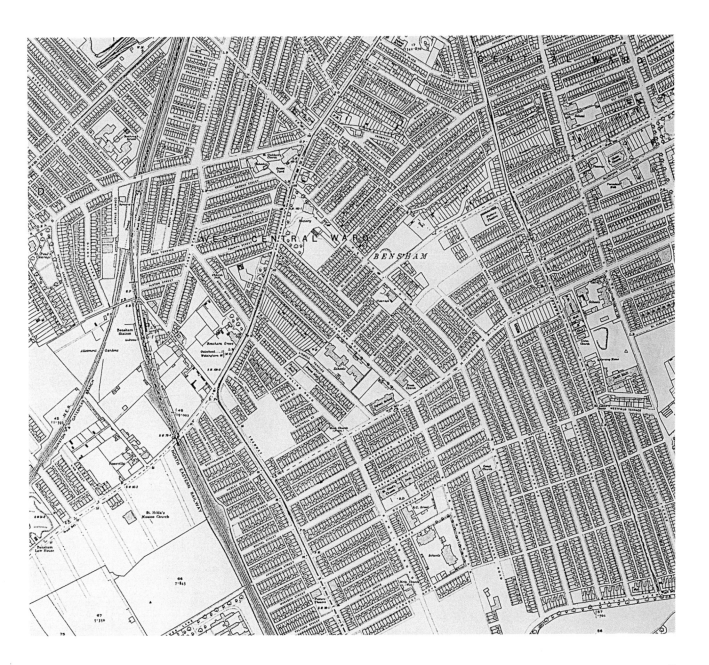

for building was usually sold on a freehold basis to developers, such as
William Affleck, in fairly large parcels, and extensive street plans were
often drawn up, it was quite common for a number of different
speculators, such as George Lucas, to be responsible for the provision
of individual houses on often quite short streets. The construction of
housing and the subsequent letting of the dwellings were seen by many
people of moderate capital, often local manufacturers and tradesmen, as
an excellent investment, providing long-term security and a useful rental
income. Dwellings were erected singly, in groups of two or three, or in
rows of up to twenty. Local building regulations, governing the size of
accommodation and sanitary arrangements, enforced a degree of
uniformity on the appearance of streets, but the staccato nature of their
development is evident on close examination: many terraces show a
number of straight joints between building phases and display many
design and decorative differences. The building material was
predominantly local brick, although some stone, usually rubble, was
used for rear walls in the earlier structures.

In October 1866 William Affleck purchased part of the Shipcote
Estate for the purpose of house building. The area between Prince
Consort Road and Alexandra Road was evidently sold on condition that
the dwelling houses built there should be of good quality and for no
more than two families to inhabit, with separate arrangements as far as
possible. This seems to be a specific directive to build what are known
as Tyneside flats, and the emphasis on separate arrangements might
have been intended to deter the practice of multi-tenanting and the
consequent overcrowding that had become characteristic of houses in
parts of the old town. A unit of Tyneside flats might at first glance
resemble conventional single-fronted terraced houses, but is in fact two
and sometimes three dwellings, one above the other, with separate front
and back doors and back yards with no internal communication
between households. Externally, they are distinguishable from normal
terrace houses by the double provision of doors, usually paired, one
opening into the ground-floor flat, the other leading to a stair rising to
the first-floor flat. The resulting elevation is quietly distinctive. Each flat
typically consisted of a heated parlour, bedroom and kitchen with a

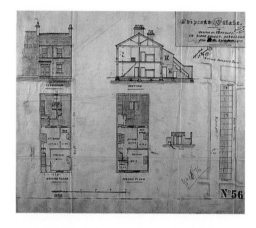

Fig 40 *Plans for a row of Tyneside flats on the south
side of Ripon Street (on the Shipcote Estate) for
George Lucas, dated 1876. The ground-floor plan
shows outdoor WCs, a great improvement on the ash
closets provided for most flats at the time.
[TWAS/T311/56/1876, reproduced by permission of
the Chief Archivist, Tyne & Wear Archives Service;
AA040377]*

Fig 41 *As they were built: Tyneside flats on the south side of Ripon Street. This street was one of plainer houses, with very simple detail around doors and windows. [AA036756]*

scullery, usually with copper (for heating water) and pantry, in a rear outshot or wing. There was a rear yard, divided into two (or three) by a brick wall, accessed from each dwelling by a back door, the upper-floor dwelling being equipped with external steps. Each dwelling was provided with either an ash or water closet and a coal house in its part of the yard. Although other areas developed flatted house types that to some extent resemble them, for example the flatted cottages built by the Edinburgh Co-operative Building Company at Stockbridge in the 1860s and the similar cottage flats developed in London, true Tyneside flats are unique to a small area, mostly Newcastle and Gateshead (they do not appear in numbers even in neighbouring Sunderland), and Bensham and Shipcote probably contain the greatest remaining concentration of good-quality examples, still doing the job they were designed to do, that is, provide a decent standard of affordable housing.

On the land he purchased Affleck laid out a series of residential streets, mostly of flatted dwellings, named after cathedral cities in England: Peterborough, Worcester, Chichester, Lichfield, Ely, Lincoln, Ripon, Exeter and Hereford. Of these, only Ripon Street, Lincoln Street, Exeter Street and Hereford Street (now called St Alban's Terrace) survive in their original form. In 1876 George Lucas received approval from the borough to erect ten flatted houses (twenty dwellings) on the south side of Ripon Street (Fig 40). They are typically built of brick and plain in appearance without front forecourts or projecting bays (Fig 41). The accommodation provided here is representative of the type of Tyneside flat built by private speculators for rent from the 1860s. Flats such as these were rented by skilled artisans, craftsmen and tradesmen. Of the seventy-eight dwellings listed in Ripon Street in 1897/8, only two were occupied by unskilled labourers, the rest by such people as policemen, engine drivers, joiners and fitters.

In 1888 a substantial tract of new building land was made available with the sale of the 28-acre (11.33-hectare) Rodsley Estate. Lying to the south of Whitehall Road, the area was laid out with a grid of streets, some existing streets being extended south into the area for development. By 1914 the area had been fully built up. Eastbourne, Westbourne and Windsor Avenues, among the earlier streets to be built,

were spaciously laid out with back lanes 16ft (4.87m) wide and cross streets 20ft (6.09m) wide, and the accommodation provided was almost exclusively in the form of Tyneside flats (Figs 42 and 43). Many terraces were built with corner shops at the intersection of cross streets (Fig 44). The terraces were built in distinct clutches by different developers, but most were designed by L H Armour, a local civil engineer. Each group of flats varied, depending on the developer, some having one- or two-storeyed projecting front window bays, either canted or rectangular, and sometimes two-roomed heated attics with dormer

Fig 42 Nos 219–25 Eastbourne Avenue. This scene is typical of the character of the former Rodsley Estate to the south of Whitehall Road. The area was developed for housing in the late 19th and early 20th centuries. [AA036782]

Fig 43 *Tyneside flats on Eastbourne Avenue. [AA036805]*

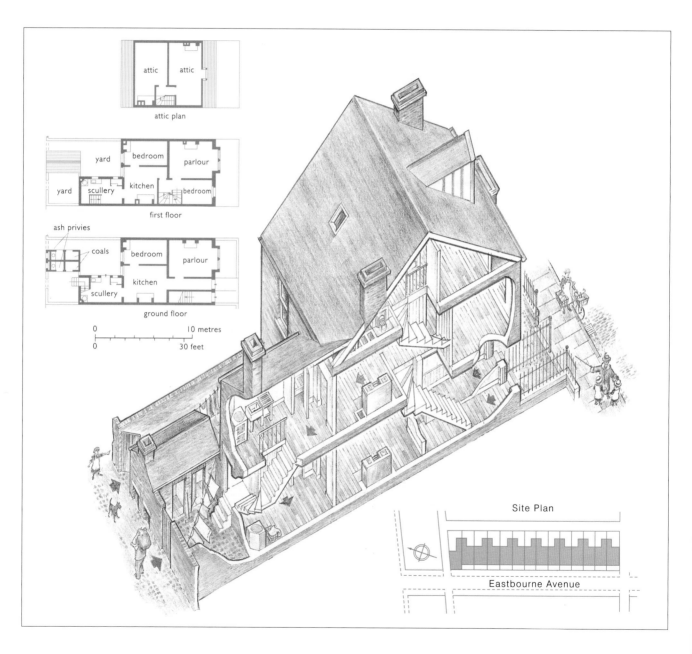

attic plan

yard | bedroom | parlour
yard | scullery | kitchen | bedroom

first floor

ash privies

coals | bedroom | parlour
scullery | kitchen

ground floor

0 ———— 10 metres
0 ———— 30 feet

Site Plan

Eastbourne Avenue

Fig 44 *(above) Tyneside flats with a corner shop on the former Rodsley Estate to the south of Whitehall Road. Many of the terraces in this area were finished with corner shops that projected forward. [AA036750]*

windows (Fig 45). Most had small forecourts with iron railings and are larger and considerably more refined than the earlier examples on Ripon Street.

From the 1860s until the outbreak of the First World War Tyneside flats dominated new housing provision. Interestingly, however, the flatted houses were relegated to the less visible parts of the area, as large and spacious self-contained houses, still built in terraces, were built along the more important streets, lending an air of elegance. The housing in Whitehall Road (1875–1911), Gladstone (1875–6), Oxford (1874–5), Cambridge (1896–1900, Fig 46) and Richmond (1876–90) Terraces was on the whole occupied by professional people such as surgeons, solicitors, accountants and engineers and by manufacturers and shopkeepers. Many were of two storeys with a basement and attic, often concealed at the front but contrived as full storeys at the rear. Self-contained houses were sometimes also built in pockets within areas otherwise dominated by flats, occasionally as the ends of terraces of flats and often built forward of the flat frontages for emphasis. In other cases pairs of flats were built in a similar way as the ends of terraces of

Fig 45 *(left) Cutaway drawing of a pair of Tyneside flats, one of fourteen pairs, including a corner shop as part of one, designed by L H Armour for Robert McKew on the east side of Eastbourne Avenue. Built in the 1890s, they were among the first in this area, and the first-floor dwelling benefited from two heated attic rooms.*

Fig 46 *(right) Cambridge Terrace. The houses here were built between 1896 and 1900 and face the earlier Oxford Terrace on the other side of the road. [AA036747]*

self-contained houses. In many of these end houses purpose-built shops occupied the ground floor.

Houses and Tyneside flats continued to be built by private landlords in Gateshead until the outbreak of the First World War in 1914 effectively put an end to all new house building. The housing shortage that followed the war forced Gateshead Council to begin building houses for rent, something it had hitherto been reluctant to do, and as it did so private developers switched to building houses for sale. In spite of their eventual demise, Tyneside flats were a success in their time, significantly reducing overcrowding and improving sanitary conditions as well as fostering a sense of community that is still valued by their inhabitants today. With the corner shops, corner pubs, places of worship and of recreation, they give Bensham a very distinctive character.

Council housing, 1918–1939

Mass housing in Gateshead before the First World War had been built by private developers for rent, and a locally unique housing type had been adopted and developed in the process. In the aftermath of the war the situation was to change as the first council houses were built and the distinctive Tyneside flat gave way to nationally standardised house forms, built with both public and private money.

The end of the First World War created a unique set of circumstances. New house building across the country had virtually ceased during the war; five million demobilised servicemen returned to civilian life; the economy had rapidly to adjust to peacetime production; and there was a genuine fear, on the part of the government, of Bolshevik revolution, since the victorious soldiers, who had suffered so greatly abroad, returned to grave problems of housing shortage and unemployment. The government's response was the 'Homes fit for Heroes' movement, embodied in two new housing acts passed in 1919. Known as the Addison Acts after Christopher Addison, president of the Local Government Board and later Minister of Health, they compelled local authorities to assess housing needs and, where needed, to build new houses for rent, something they had already been empowered nationally to do at their own discretion since 1890. A Housing Manual was issued, based on the Tudor Waters report of 1918, recommending variations on two main house types, those with a living room but no parlour and those with both. All were to have a scullery, larder, coal store and a bath (either in a bathroom or in the scullery) and an indoor WC. Housing estates were to be thoughtfully laid out to create beautiful vistas, and variety was to be provided by the arrangement of different house types and styles. Trees, grassed areas and shrubbery were also recommended to create a pleasant, semi-rural feel.

The Addison Acts prompted a wave of suburban council-house building throughout Britain, and Gateshead Council, for so long opposed to building houses itself because of the vested interests of many councillors and ratepayers, was forced to act. One in three people in Gateshead was still living in overcrowded conditions (the old town-centre slums still existed), compared to one in eleven nationally, and in March 1919 the first Council Housing Committee met to examine the problem. It was the beginning of a continuing struggle to house the borough's expanding population, juggling slum clearance with new house and flat building.

In 1919 it was estimated that 1,950 houses would be needed in Gateshead within the next three years. The initial response was the planning of a new estate of 360 houses, with a density of twelve houses per acre (per 0.4046 hectare), at a 30-acre (12.14-hectare) site at Carr Hill. The inadequacy of this scheme was highlighted when it became clear that no other authority in the region was planning a scheme of fewer than 600 houses (Newcastle was proposing 5,000). The Committee hastily revised its proposal to 650 houses at ten per acre. Even so, the scheme was rejected by the Ministry of Health until it was pointed out that this was merely the first instalment of a much larger proposal not yet finalised. In July 1919 Richard Wylie RIBA was appointed to lay out the new estate and build the houses. Work began, but in July 1921, with 202 houses underway, there was a national withdrawal of subsidy for council houses by the Ministry of Health.

Fig 47 *Aerial view of the first phase of the Carr Hill Council Housing Scheme. Hodkin Park, named after the first chairman of the Council Housing Committee, is on the right of the picture. [NMR17753/23]*

The 202 were completed in 1922 and permission was granted by the Ministry for a further 30 houses to infill spaces and finish the first phase of the estate (Fig 47). By the time that this was achieved, at the end of 1923, the number of new houses needed in the borough had been re-estimated at 2,830.

The first 232 houses built at Carr Hill broadly adhered to the standard government specifications but with variations (Figs 48, 49 and 50). The estate had a main street (Broadway) curving through the centre, three cross streets (The Avenue, Pottersway and Crossway) and a few culs-de-sac to fill the angles. Both non-parlour and parlour houses were built as semi-detached pairs or in terraces of four or eight with covered passages, one for each pair of houses, to provide access to rear gardens. Terrace-end houses were treated as pavilions and often projected forward, and were usually distinguished by steep gables or hips to the street, as were some centre-terrace houses. All houses had, on the ground floor, a living room fitted with a cooking range, a scullery with gas cooker, a larder and a coal store; most had three bedrooms on the first floor, although a small number of four-bedroomed houses were also built. All had a bath and a WC, usually on the ground floor, and the coal store had an external delivery chute unless there was internal access to it near the back door. Facilities for the community were limited: a proposed community hall does not seem to have been built, nor, in this first phase, were any shops, places of worship or schools.

Between 1923 and 1927 Carr Hill was expanded with the construction of a further 342 houses and 7 estate shops, and a new estate of 204 houses was developed at Bensham. Both schemes used direct and contracted labour. The new houses at Carr Hill and Bensham had accommodation similar to those of the first phase at Carr Hill, although this time electricity was supplied and each house had an electric rather than a gas cooker in the scullery. They were, however, markedly different in character and appearance from the earlier houses at Carr Hill (Fig 51). Almost all were semi-detached pairs and only two terraces of four houses were built, on Broadway at Carr Hill. A harder type of red brick was used for the new houses and many were rendered on the first floor. At the Bensham estate a number of houses were built

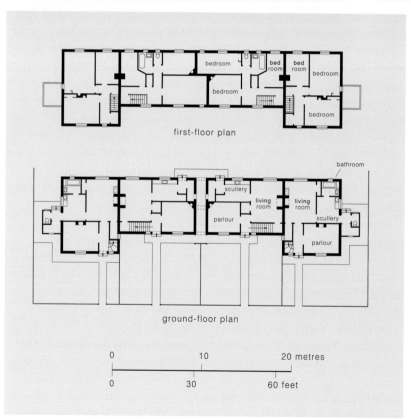

first-floor plan

bathroom

scullery

living room

living room

parlour

scullery

parlour

ground-floor plan

bedroom

bed room

bed room

bedroom

bedroom

bedroom

0   10   20 metres

0   30   60 feet

Fig 48 *(above left) Nos 32–4 Broadway were among the earliest houses to be built at Carr Hill, in the early 1920s. [AA035289]*

Fig 49 *(above right) Spaciously laid-out houses in Ermine Crescent, part of the first phase of the Carr Hill Estate. [AA035288]*

Fig 50 *A terrace of four houses on Pottersway, typical of many built during the first phase of the Carr Hill Estate.*

of artificial stone rubble, interspersed with the standard brick-built equivalents for variation. Stone or concrete lintels were built into all window openings and projecting central or end bays usually had gablets bearing a simple cross motif in raised brick. Different styles of house were often built in alternating pairs to avoid oppressive uniformity but retain the elegance of symmetry. Low concrete panel fencing was erected around front gardens and, as with the first phase, the new streets were well planted with trees.

As well as developing its estates during the 1920s, the council also sought to address its obligation to clear the 'unhealthy areas' of the town,

Fig 51 *Ascot Crescent, Bensham, built in the mid-1920s. The houses here are similar to those used to extend the Carr Hill Estate. [AA036531]*

close to the river, where overcrowding and the consequent risk of
disease was at its worst. The council did not consider the inhabitants of
such areas to be suitable tenants for the new estate houses, even if they
were able to afford the rents asked, and alternative low-cost housing had
to be provided. The clearance of Cannon Street, for example, resulted in
the construction of three blocks of flats, each of three storeys and since
demolished, in the Albany Road area of Saltmeadows.

From 1927 to 1939 Gateshead Council continued to build houses in
an attempt to combat the persistent shortage, developing the Field
House Estate at the end of the 1920s and building new estates at Lobley
Hill, Old Fold, Wrekenton and Deckham Hall. The last was begun in

Fig 52 *Aerial view of the Deckham Hall Estate.*
[NMR17753/21]

Fig 53 *Kingston Road, Deckham Hall Estate, built between 1936 and 1939. The houses on this estate were plainer in appearance than those at Carr Hill or Bensham and were built to a higher density. [AA036521]*

1936 (by which time Gateshead Council had erected 2,360 houses) and was finished by 1939. It was built by the specially created North Eastern Housing Association, to which responsibility for housing was delegated, and was laid out as a series of irregular concentric rings (Fig 52). The houses were of very uniform appearance compared with those built at Carr Hill and Bensham. Orange brick was used throughout and less attention was given to landscaping, with only a few green spaces and evidently no tree planting, producing an austere effect overall (Fig 53). Houses were either semi-detached, built in terraces of four or as flats in pairs of two. Pairs of semi-detached houses of L-shaped plan were built to flank the few semicircular green spaces that were provided. The accommodation was broadly similar to that of the earlier estate houses, but a large number of two-bedroomed houses were also built.

Even though it ultimately failed to solve the problem of housing shortage, the public provision of housing between the wars represents a considerable achievement. Dogged from the start by the slow process of government approval, which inevitably led to piecemeal development, house building continually lagged behind demand. The situation was exacerbated by the council's tendency to cherry-pick its tenants: the relatively high rents that it charged also acted to exclude those worst affected by the overcrowding the estates were meant to solve. Council provision for the poorest classes, in the form of flats and tenement blocks, was probably little better than the slums they replaced, a fact reflected by their limited survival. Nevertheless, Gateshead's inter-war housing programmes represent a large-scale investment designed to address the need to create a better environment for the poorer levels of society. The well-planned estates at Carr Hill and Bensham are attractive, good examples of 1920s garden suburbs, and must have made a dramatic impact when first built. Providing a consistent standard of building as well as a spacious and airy setting, the housing contrasted starkly with the town-centre slums as well as the regimented pre-war terraces of Bensham and Shipcote. The later change of emphasis and decline in architectural quality, represented by the high-density and less attractive Deckham Hall Estate of the 1930s, reflects the more utilitarian attitudes to housing that dominated the decade before the Second World War. Quantity with austerity and economy were once again the governing forces.

Public and private housing after the Second World War

Britain's housing stock suffered enormous damage during the Second World War, although Gateshead was not too badly affected. New house building had once again ground to a halt, and 200,000 homes were destroyed and three million were damaged by enemy action. The prospect of peace signalled the need to rebuild, and in 1944 the Dudley Report, like the Tudor Walters report before it, proposed new national standards for post-war houses, published in a new Housing Manual. The Labour Party's victory in the General Election of July 1945 saw Britain seized by a fresh climate of social idealism, epitomised by the creation of the 'welfare state'. The new government was determined not to repeat the mistakes of the inter-war years, but to provide better quality houses and environments not just by building more suburban estates of the inter-war type but also by promoting the regeneration of existing decayed urban centres and by the building of entirely new towns with an artificially engineered social mix.

In Gateshead overcrowding was once again a big problem. Many people from areas that had been bombed came to Gateshead to live with friends and relatives, a substantial number of whom lived in areas targeted for clearance as unhealthy slums. By 1942 there were 5,620 people living in properties scheduled for demolition. When the war ended, Gateshead Council at once set to work building new houses, and the first new estates, at Highfield and Blue Quarries, had been completed by 1948. By the end of 1950 the large Beacon Lough Estate of 347 houses had also been completed, at a cost of £542,490. Spaciously laid out on the western slopes of Gateshead Fell, Beacon Lough is typical of the large brick-built cottage estates constructed in many parts of the country in the years immediately after the war (Figs 54 and 55). With its numerous winding side roads and culs-de-sac, it was recognised by the Minister of Health as one of the best laid out housing estates in the country.

Where Beacon Lough was a large and sprawling low-density housing estate, the fifty-nine-house Cedars Green Estate, built in the years 1952–4 at a cost of £87,000, was small, discrete and unobtrusive, arranged around two roughly circular greens on the former grounds of a large private house. The same house types as at Beacon Lough were used, and the estate adopted the same principles of spacious layout and attractive landscaping (Fig 56). But Cedars Green was evidently always intended as a prestigious development and came to be regarded locally as proof that a council estate could be 'Utopia', since it was peaceful, secluded and select but not impersonal, remote or cut-off. Its low density, however, meant that it made a very small contribution to the

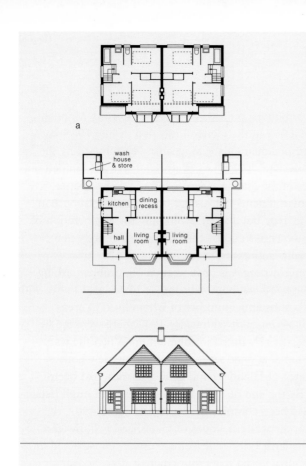

a

wash
house
& store

kitchen | dining
recess

hall | living
room | living
room

front elevation

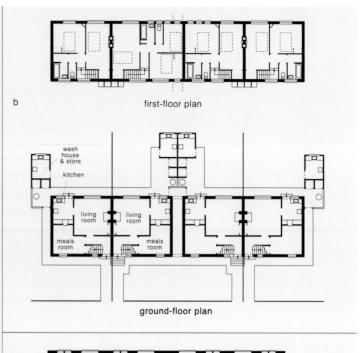

b

first-floor plan

wash
house
& store

kitchen

living
room | living
room

meals
room | meals
room

ground-floor plan

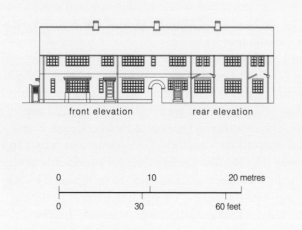

0   10   20 metres

0   30   60 feet

c

first-floor plan

wash
house
& store

kitchen | kitchen

meals
recess | meals
room

living
room | living
room

hall | hall

ground-floor plan

Fig 54 *(left) Three types of houses built at Beacon Lough in the late 1940s.*

Fig 55 *(right) Torver Place, Beacon Lough Estate. These council houses were built in the late 1940s.* [AA037003]

Fig 56 *The council houses at Cedars Green were built in the years 1952–4. They were of the same type as those at Beacon Lough, but the estate was much smaller.* [AA037013]

overall provision of housing in Gateshead and, not surprisingly, it was the only estate of its type to be built in the town. Ironically, its completion coincided with that of the colossal 1,372-home neighbourhood unit at Wrekenton.

By 1954 Britain was in the grip of a major shortage of traditional building materials, especially bricks, which had a significant effect on Gateshead's ability to fulfil its housing programme. In response, a number of concrete houses were included in the council's plans between 1952 and 1954. At first these were very modest: an 'Orlit' block of eighteen flats was built in Saltwell Road (Fig 57), for example, and 150 'Dorran' semi-detached houses were constructed in Rose Street, Carr Hill Road, at Black Hill and elsewhere (Fig 58). This was at a time, however, when the use of concrete for mass housing, inspired by Le Corbusier's Unité d'Habitation at Marseille (1946–52), was rapidly becoming very popular among planners. Many British housing authorities embarked upon ambitious and futuristic concrete-based housing schemes, some of the best being Roehampton Park (1952–5), by the London County Council Department of Architecture, and Park Hill (1957–60), by Sheffield City Corporation Architect's Department. Gateshead soon followed the trend, and from the mid-1950s and through the 1960s the council, encouraged by the Housing Subsidies Act of 1956, wholeheartedly embraced the concept of 'modern' high-rise housing. All the major housing schemes of the period were designed 'in-house' by the staff of the Borough Architect's Department, which, under the leadership of A Leslie Berry and separated from the surveyor's and planner's department, gained something of a nationwide reputation for innovation and quality, attracting many budding young architects.

The new building schemes were combined with a vigorous programme of slum clearance: by 1970 Gateshead topped the league table of local authorities in the North in this respect. The visual and emotional impact of the new tower blocks on a population used to living in and among small traditional brick houses must have been immense, and many were delighted with the novel way of living, high up in clean modern homes rather than tired old slums. High-rise housing was

Fig 57 *Concrete 'Orlit' flats on Saltwell Road, built between 1952 and 1954 at a time when traditional building materials were in short supply. [AA038431]*

Fig 58 *Six semi-detached concrete 'Dorran' houses on Rose Street, built between 1952 and 1954. [AA038436]*

expensive compared with the earlier traditional housing, the first completed scheme (196 dwellings in four blocks at Barn Close) costing an appreciable £548,141 11s 6d. Another major problem was the legacy of so many years of coal mining beneath the town, which made large areas of land simply unsuitable for tower-block building. Between 1955 and 1965 this resulted in a series of large but mostly scattered blocks being individually conceived, rather than a slew of large multi-towered estates (Fig 59a–d). The Barn Close blocks were completed in 1956 and were followed by Priory Court (1957), Regent Court (1958) and the Chandless slum-clearance redevelopment (1960–3). The last was a true estate replacing an area of decaying 19th-century terraced houses (Fig 60). It consisted of three sixteen-storeyed slab blocks, a number of four-storeyed maisonette blocks and some aged persons' bungalows. It eventually included a shop, pub, children's play area and infants' school. The slab blocks were equipped with under-floor heating and are notable for having been constructed from the inside outwards and upwards, without the need for scaffolding, a technique pioneered in Sweden and Denmark and developed for use in Gateshead by the Borough Architect's Department. It was subsequently used elsewhere in the borough. Chandless was followed by Bensham Court in 1964 and a pair of twenty-one-storeyed slab blocks at the Teams slum-clearance redevelopment area in 1965.

That year was a milestone in the history of council housing in Gateshead. The council achieved its goal of building 1,000 houses in a year, and the 10,000th council dwelling in the borough was constructed. It also saw the start of the rapid exploitation of the remaining open land in the south. At the same time, however, there emerged a realisation of the physical and sociological problems caused by unrelieved high-rise living. As well as the nationally recognised problems of individual isolation (when, in 1964, a man died alone in his Chandless flat his body was not discovered for three weeks) and poor community spirit, some specific local problems had emerged. For example, a lack of outdoor play facilities at Barn Close meant that the communal corridors became overrun by raucous children, from families living both in the flats and elsewhere, and its bad name led to a boycott by those on the

a

b

Fig 59 *Towers of Gateshead:*
(a) Barn Close: 196 dwellings were provided in four T-shaped blocks with communal roof-top walking areas, built 1955/6 [AA038454];
(b) Bensham Court, built in 1964 [AA038435];
(c) Redheugh Court, one of two twenty-one-storeyed slab blocks at Teams built in 1965 [AA038445]; and
(d) Regent Court, built in 1958 [AA038471].

Fig 60 *(above, bottom) Chandless, a slum-clearance redevelopment of 1960–3. The estate was dominated by three sixteen-storeyed slab blocks but also included many four-storeyed maisonette blocks and some aged-persons' bungalows. [AA038463]*

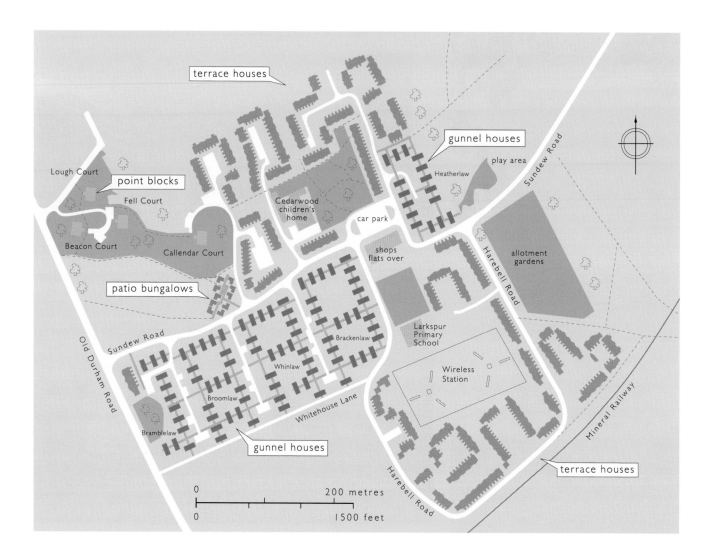

Fig 61 *Plan of Beacon Lough East. The estate, which was built in the years 1965–7, mixed low-rise semi-detached and terrace housing with four point blocks and a number of aged persons' bungalows. It was described as a 'safe estate' because vehicle and pedestrian circulation routes were segregated.*

housing list; Priory Court was plagued by beetles breeding in the heating pipes; certain tenants of Regent Court took to fouling the building's lifts; and Bensham Court, controversial from the outset due to the known existence of underground mine workings, was persistently plagued by rumours that it was sinking. Despite the council's assertions to the contrary (and presumably the visual evidence), it retained a bad reputation and was not popular (it was also said to create an artificial down-draught, which made it impossible to light fires in some of the older traditional houses that stood in its shadow).

A change in approach is evident in the design of a new estate to the east of the Old Durham Road, when a 68.5-acre (27.7-hectare) site was utilised to provide for a much more balanced community (Fig 61). Built in four phases from 1965 to 1967, it consisted of 4 point blocks (Figs 62 and 63), 196 flat-roofed concrete 'gunnel' houses (Figs 64 and 65), 515 brick cross-wall terrace houses (Fig 66), 30 patio bungalows for the elderly, a children's home, primary school, pub and shops. The different types of houses on the estate, which adhered rigidly to the strict standards specified in the Parker Morris *Homes for Today and Tomorrow* report of 1961, were designed to overcome the problem posed by abandoned mine working and complement the existing landscape. The layout of the estate segregated pedestrian and vehicular circulation routes, making the environment safer for families and children. Named Beacon Lough East, the idiosyncratic estate proved a success; it was popular with tenants and won a commendation in the government's award scheme 'Good Design in Housing 1968'. It was followed by the similarly designed Harlow Green and Allerdene 'Safety' Estates (Fig 67), built hard up to the borough's southern boundary, effectively exhausting the supply of fresh building land.

As Beacon Lough East was nearing completion, two new and rather different housing schemes, designed to offer a high-density alternative to high-rise blocks, were in preparation. The evident problems associated with high-rise living, which put off prospective tenants, combined with the slow rate of new house building, which did not match the rate of slum clearance, had worsened the housing problem. The shortage of houses, the council believed, was the reason for a significant decline in

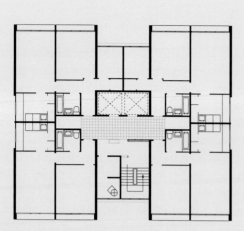

typical floor plan

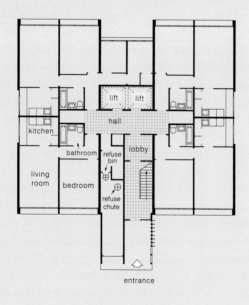

lift | lift

hall

kitchen

bathroom | refuse bin | lobby

living room | bedroom

refuse chute

entrance

ground-floor plan

0 — 10 metres

0 — 30 feet

Fig 62 *(left) Plan of a point block, Beacon Lough East.*

Fig 63 *(above) Fell Court, Lough Court and Beacon Court. Three of the four twelve-storeyed point blocks at Beacon Lough East, each containing forty-eight flats. [AA038477]*

Fig 64 *(below) Heatherlaw, a footpath at Beacon Lough East with bridging 'gunnel' houses. [AA038486]*

Fig 65 *(right) Cutaway drawing of semi-detached 'gunnel' houses at Beacon Lough East. The term 'gunnel' refers to the public passage that passed through each pair of houses.*

Fig 66 *Terrace houses on Sundew Road, Beacon Lough East. [AA038483]*

Fig 67 *Harewood Green and Bedale and Acomb Courts, Harlow Green Estate. At the extreme southern edge of the borough, the estate has views over open countryside. [AA038496]*

Fig 68 *St Cuthbert's Village was built in the late 1960s but, beset by problems, was demolished in the 1990s, except for St Cuthbert's Court – the point block – and a concrete footbridge across Askew Road (seen here from Kyloe Walk). [AA038452]*

the population of central Gateshead during the mid-1960s, as young people moved to other areas in search of affordable homes. With this in mind, the 'village' concept was adopted for the St Cuthbert's Road and Clasper Street schemes, both slum clearance areas and both meant to be part of a wider urban renewal programme intended to link Barn Close with the outlying Teams development. Both had been completed by 1972.

The first, St Cuthbert's Village, was built on the steep north-facing slopes of Windmill Hills and straddled Askew Road (Fig 68). It was intended to be an entirely self-contained village of 3,500 people and consisted of a maze of low- and medium-rise linking 'scissor blocks' with roof gardens, on either side of Askew Road, radiating from the centre and linked by numerous communal walkways and steps around open communal areas. There was to be a single seventeen-storeyed point block; facilities for cars were to be limited; and it was intended mainly for young single people and couples. It was thought that living in such a close communal environment would enable people to make friends with each other easily and that the isolation associated with tower blocks would be avoided. St Cuthbert's Village was intended to be a bold and pioneering showpiece development, unlike anything that had gone before in Gateshead, and it was opened with great ceremony by Prime Minister Harold Wilson in 1970, having cost £3,700,000. By contrast, Clasper Village was a much simpler affair and very different. Although the site was level, old mine workings again limited the type of houses that could be built and designers restricted the development to a type of detached low-rise cluster block of two-and-a-half storeys, each of eight dwellings (Fig 69).

Although contemporary, the two 'villages' could not have been more different. St Cuthbert's Village was never popular: the houses were occupied long before any amenities were provided and residents said they felt marooned; the young never materialised in the numbers expected, and elderly people moved in instead. The close-proximity living, far from encouraging people to make friends as had been hoped, led to squabbles and feuds while much of the estate became a haven for rats and vandals. The type of ceiling heating provided in most dwellings, which was seen as the heating system of the future and expected to have the advantage of providing instant heat when switched on, but with running costs equal to or even less than those of under-floor or block storage heating, was quite inadequate and many homes were cold and damp. In addition, a number of the ground-floor houses were terraced into the hillside, which meant that there was no ventilation in the sculleries and so food rapidly went bad. In the early 1990s St Cuthbert's Village was finally demolished, except for the point block and a concrete footbridge across Askew Road, and is conspicuous as the only major failure among the many council-housing schemes in Gateshead. The more intimate scale of Clasper Village, on the other hand, proved popular, and accommodation there has always been in high demand; it remains an attractive and well-maintained residential unit. It is not surprising that the next housing development in Gateshead, at Sunderland Road (1973), and many subsequently used modestly sized linking blocks, similar in appearance to the Clasper Village blocks, as well as a pair of twelve-storeyed point blocks and seven shops in a precinct.

While Gateshead Council was building St Cuthbert's and Clasper Villages, across the River Team, in Dunston, Whickham Council was seeking to address the same problem of high-density housing supply without resorting to profligate high-rise development. The result was a linear concrete estate of four-storeyed blocks, of flats and maisonettes, and one point block. It was built in 1969 and was designed by Owen Luder Associates, also responsible for the Trinity Square shopping centre and car park in Gateshead. The centrepiece of the estate was Derwent Tower, an idiosyncratic, twenty-nine-storeyed point block of 196 flats (Fig 70). It is shaped like a cog with a narrow stem-like base, set within a large concrete basin giving access to the tower's services, including pumps for use in the event of the River Team flooding. Because the base is so much narrower than the main structure, the whole has to be supported by large concrete fin-like flying buttresses, a feature that has earned the building the alias of 'The Rocket'. The design is unique in Britain, and inevitably divides opinion, and is unlike anything built by

Fig 69 *Cluster blocks at Palmerston Walk, Clasper Village. Each block contained four ground-floor flats with four maisonettes above. [AA038439]*

Fig 70 *Derwent Tower (196 flats) was designed by Owen Luder and built in 1969. The concrete basin at the bottom was intended to overcome the potential problem of floodwater from the River Team. It is unique in Britain and it is easy to see why it is known locally as 'The Rocket'. [AA038514]*

Gateshead Council, although it is now part of the borough's housing stock.

The final chapter in the history of housing in Gateshead tells an interesting story, one reflecting many changing outlooks. By the mid-1970s the British economy's heavy-industrial base had virtually collapsed and local-authority house building had come to an end. A new era and philosophy were ushered in with the election of Margaret Thatcher's Conservative Government in 1979; henceforth it was the private sector that was seen as the engine of change and the provider of housing, and home ownership was seen as a major social objective. In Gateshead, pockets of traditionally styled housing sprang up on the remaining vacant land and on 'brownfield' sites (previously developed urban, commercial or industrial land now suitable for redevelopment). Examples include Festival Park (Fig 71), built on the site of Norwood Coking Plant (later part of the National Garden Festival of 1990), and Tyne Views, the redevelopment of the site of St Cuthbert's Village at Windmill Hills (Fig 72). The wheel, however, is still turning, and medium- and high-rise housing, formerly so controversial on council estates, is now re-emerging, in the form of luxury apartments at Baltic Quay (*see* Fig 34) and, to designs by Wayne and Gerardine Hemingway, near Dunston Staiths. The change is an indication of how the town is facing up to a future in the post-industrial age.

Fig 72 *Tyne Views, Windmill Hills, and the earlier St Cuthbert's Court. This development of the late 20th century and the early 21st is on the site of the ill-fated St Cuthbert's Village. [AA038450]*

Fig 71 *(left) Red Admiral Court, Festival Park. The Park was built in the 1990s on the site of Norwood Coking Plant following its use for the National Garden Festival of 1990. [AA038476]*

CHAPTER 4

Conservation and change in urban Gateshead

The borough of Gateshead contains within its boundaries landscapes of great variety. The town itself has a dramatic river frontage to the Tyne, overlooking Newcastle, and behind this are distinctive commercial, industrial and residential areas, the last showing different stages in the development of housing over the last two centuries. Around the town are villages and rural areas with some outstanding architecture: the 18th-century country house of Gibside with its chapel in a stunning landscape setting, the remains of the 14th-century Ravensworth Castle and the 18th-century Axwell Park. The remains of industry are apparent over much of the borough, in a landscape formerly dominated by coal mining: the mines have gone, but Dunston Staiths and the mining villages of Clara Vale and Marley Hill remain as monuments to the 'black gold' that first brought national prominence to Tyneside. This is in addition to an older heritage represented by some of the borough's Scheduled Ancient Monuments, such as the Roman Washingwell Fort and the medieval fortified hall house at Old Holinside.

The subject of this book is the less spectacular aspects of the legacy of the past, and the focus is very much upon the town rather than upon the borough as a whole. Earlier chapters have shown that some parts of this legacy – the Team Valley Trading Estate, the concentration of Tyneside flats in Bensham, the recent cultural facilities – are of wide interest and importance, and that much of it – the public buildings, schools, 20th-century housing – has undoubted local significance and meaning, forming what has been described as 'the familiar and cherished local scene': although these parts may be regarded as a historic commonplace, they are valued precisely because they are the background to the highs and lows of everyday life in the town. Recent research, expressed in the review of the historic environment published as *Power of Place* (English Heritage 2000), and government policy, outlined in *The Historic Environment: A Force for our Future* (DCMS 2001), demonstrate the importance of the everyday aspects of our urban and rural landscapes in giving areas a unique identity, in fostering local pride and in contributing to successful and sustainable communities.

All aspects of the historic environment change continually: it is impossible to fossilise the past. Present-day needs and aspirations act on what has been left to us from earlier ages to produce a new reality (Fig 73), sometimes subtly blending ancient and modern, sometimes entirely sweeping away buildings and areas that have no part to play in the future. We see these forces at work in Gateshead today as the town adjusts to the challenges of the 21st century. There is a demand for continuing economic and employment development, much of this dependent upon physical regeneration of 'brownfield sites' and on redevelopment of commercial areas. Government policy on housing will increase the pressure on urban areas, raising population density there to reduce new development in the countryside. Strong pressures for economic and cultural development in the Tyne Corridor (Fig 74) and the need for town-centre renewal (Fig 75) will intensify pressure throughout the built-up areas of the borough.

Conservation has an important role in the challenges facing Gateshead today. There is wide acceptance that economic change in itself will not create towns and cities where people wish to live and work. The historic environment will help to shape the future, not only because it represents a valuable economic resource, but also because it provides a strong sense of identity, so important in our commitment to the places where we spend our time. Within Gateshead Council, a small team of conservation staff ensures that the historic environment forms a part of major policy documents, such as the Gateshead Unitary Development Plan.

Protection of the historic environment takes different forms, and it is interesting to study which aspects of the environment have been recognised as being of special interest. The listed buildings within Gateshead's urban area include the town's oldest and best churches, a fine early 19th-century terrace of houses (Walker Terrace), Sir Joseph Swan's house in Kells Lane (the first house in England to be wired for domestic electrical lighting) and, last but not least, Robert Stephenson's stupendous High Level Bridge over the Tyne. The list of grade II structures includes fourteen Victorian street monuments or fountains, ten suburban churches (all Victorian), four pubs, nine public buildings

Fig 73 *George Black's 'Palace' on Sunderland Road, a 1,450-seat cinema and theatre of 1909, which closed in 1960. Its future must be uncertain, since slum clearance and redevelopment schemes, and the building of major new roads, have left the building isolated and forgotten in a forlorn cul-de-sac. The cinema survives in an urban landscape utterly different in character from the bustling Edwardian neighbourhood in which it was originally situated. [AA038601]*

Fig 74 *The Sage Gateshead and Tyne bridges. In contrast to the redundant and isolated Palace cinema, The Sage Gateshead, an international centre for music designed by Norman Foster and built in the years 2000–4, is a striking example of a purpose-built contemporary cultural facility in a zone of carefully planned waterfront regeneration. [DP003370]*

Fig 75 *Trinity Square shopping precinct was designed in the mid-1960s and replaced much of Gateshead's old town centre. Very much a period piece, its brutal concrete environments are not sympathetic to 21st-century tastes and many shop units lie empty. [DP000119]*

(including the handsome Shipley Art Gallery of 1914–17) and thirteen commercial or industrial buildings. Domestic architecture is represented by about twenty detached houses, including Saltwell Towers, the industrialist William Wailes's grand house of 1871 and nine separate Victorian terraces. A pair of Tyneside flats on Fife Street – nos 33 and 35 – is listed 'as perhaps the last surviving unspoilt example of a local 2-flat dwelling of high quality but modest size, in a polite style and formerly in a polite setting'; this is the only pair of listed Tyneside flats in Gateshead, or anywhere else in the North-East. Tyneside flats are of considerable interest and significance, having once been the dominant type of terraced dwellings throughout the conurbation north and south of the river. As is indicated in Chapter 3, more such dwellings could survive in Gateshead than elsewhere on the Tyne, and although further listing is not considered necessary, the importance of the resource in Gateshead should be reflected in local conservation policies.

The designation of individual buildings (listing) is complemented by the borough's twenty-two conservation areas. Conservation area designation is concerned with the overall historic character of a place (rather than, for instance, the interior of buildings) and provides an appropriate management tool for landscapes rather than buildings. Some of Gateshead's conservation areas protect the best of the borough's parks and gardens, reflecting the important role that these have played in the life of the town. Seven conservation areas lie within the main urban area that was the subject of this study. Four are based around the housing of the Saltwell, Low Fell, Chowdene and Sheriff Hill areas. These contain a great diversity of housing, mainly from the 19th century, and cover a range of urban landscapes, including some of the housing stock that forms the subject of part of this book. One conservation area comprises just two listed terraces (Regent Street and Walker Terrace), and the Bridges conservation area covers the original historic core of Gateshead and its dramatic railway infrastructure. The last conservation area is centred on Coatsworth Road, the heart of Bensham. Although this is a relatively small conservation area, it contains a number of terraces ranging in date from the early to the late 19th century.

Some aspects of the town's housing stock (as well as parks and gardens, Fig 76) are, therefore, represented among its listed buildings and conservation areas. In addition to these forms of recognition, the council's 'Hidden Treasures' project, which invited the people of Gateshead to suggest buildings for inclusion on a non-statutory 'Local' list of buildings of special interest, may identify whether pre-1914 terraced housing and other housing types are valued by the local community. The Local List will supplement the statutory list and represents a positive step towards evaluating and retaining what in the local scene is important to the people who live and work there. Because it is confined to individual buildings or short terraces rather than large groups, a Local List is unable to provide recognition for valued local areas, but the consultative process by which it is being compiled will help to identify which areas matter to people.

The council is examining ways in which it can recognise the special architectural and historic character of such larger areas of housing or townscape that have a discernible quality and value but which would not fit the criteria for designation as a conservation area.

The values placed on everyday aspects of the historic environment will be at the centre of the debate on the future of our heritage. Neither English Heritage nor Gateshead Council advocates the wholesale extension of designation or the development of new forms of control. There is no desire to fossilise the whole town of Gateshead: this would not be in anybody's interests. Instead, planning must be based on good assessment of the resource. Studies such as the one provided in this book are essential in evaluating and understanding the making of the urban landscape. This understanding is a starting point in determining what matters, in national and local terms, and, conversely, where the best opportunities for change lie. Where a resource has local significance, then a case can be made for conservation within much-needed schemes of renewal. In this context, conservation is as much about mediating social and economic change as it is about the protection of valued physical fabric.

In any programme of regeneration, we now recognise that success will flow not from crude and insensitive clearances, such as

Fig 76 *Saltwell Park (listed grade II, Register of Parks and Gardens) began as private gardens in the 1850s but has served the recreational needs of the people of Gateshead as a public park for well over a century. Although parts of the park have been remodelled several times, it retains many enhancing early features, such as the restored pavilion, originally of 1880, seen here. [DP000117]*

characterised renewal in the 1960s, or from dogmatic assertion that nothing must change. Solutions lie in policies that represent local aspirations for a better standard of living within an environment that reflects the area's distinctive evolution. Partnership – of local and national agencies and including the views of local people – will be the key to success, and both English Heritage and Gateshead Council will join to work for the best results. Conservation, now a sophisticated and sensitive tool, will play a dynamic role in enhancing resources that can act as anchors or stabilisers and reflect local people's pride in their neighbourhoods.

Bibliographical note

The research for this book included an examination of a wide range of sources. The principal source was, of course, the surviving buildings and landscape of Gateshead, and fieldwork resulted in notes on, and small- and medium-format photographs of, selected monuments and areas in the town. Primary documentary sources included historic maps and photographs, building control registers and plans, trade directories, contemporary newspaper reports and council records. The evidence of documents was supplemented by material drawn from published sources: the most important publications are listed here as a guide to further reading.

Addyman, J and Fawcett, B 1999 *The High Level Bridge and Newcastle Central Station: 150 Years Across the Tyne*. Newcastle upon Tyne: North Eastern Railway Association

Loebl, H 1988 *Government Factories and the Origins of British Regional Policy, 1934–1948: Including a Case Study of North Eastern Trading Estates Ltd*. Aldershot: Avebury

McCord, N 1979 *North East England: An Economic and Social History*. London: Batsford

Manders, F W D 1973 *A History of Gateshead*. Gateshead: Gateshead Corporation

Manders, F 1995 *Cinemas of Gateshead*. Gateshead: MBC

Pevsner, N and Williamson, E 1983 *County Durham*. Harmondsworth: Penguin Books

Rogers, F 1974 *Gateshead: An Early Victorian Boom Town*. Wallsend: Priory Press

Turnbull, L and Womack, S [1978] *Home Sweet Home: A Look at Housing in the North East from 1800–1977*. Gateshead: Gateshead Metropolitan Borough Council Department of Education

Front cover Town Hall, West Street. [DP00046]
Inside front cover Derwent Tower, 'The Rocket', Dunston. [AA038508]
Back cover 'Designing', 'Estimating', 'Building', frieze within the former headquarters building of North Eastern Trading Estates Ltd, Team Valley. [AA0028900]
Back flap The Sage Gateshead, Gateshead Quays. [DP003371]
Inside back cover Gateshead location map.